I0516901

SO WE PRACTICE

GANDY DANCER PRESS

Also by Todd Griese

Poetry

North Fork
Spiritual Lines

Audio Compilation

No Work, No Food
(with Terry Bozzio)

SO WE PRACTICE

TODD GRIESE

GANDY DANCER PRESS

Published by Gandy Dancer Press, Camarillo, CA
in association with Blue Jay Ink, Ojai, California

Copyright © 2023, Todd Griese
All rights reserved
Printed in the United States of America

ISBN: 978-1-959457-15-2

Cover art: Detail of a Porcelain Throng-Back Screen,
Qing Dynasty.

Inset art: Detail of Porcelain Throng-Back Screen,
Qing Dynasty.

Cover design: Dave Reeser, Blue Jay Ink.

CONTENTS

For Christine
Une rivière d'esprit et d'amour

ARROWHEAD

The sun settling
    in the puddle
out beyond the stripped down
    barren and diseased
pines that hold the
    disorder within.
Buttressed, here on this bank
    of negativity and resistance
lies an arrowhead in praise
of a soft and noble heart.

Remember to breathe after
    getting out of water
open the flow and affirm the gift.
Child of God
    judged to be loved
and having the capacity
    to not struggle in the struggle.
The logic of faith seeps in
    it wasn't conjured up
and it won't tire you out.
It floats.

    It floats the misty fog
    on the cresting waves
as seen from this vantage here, high
on the damp matted grass of gentle slope.
    Answers to questions pillowed
    in the absence of form and
pushed with intent along the fog line

An arrow is only as strong
as its bow, put one foot in front
of the other, pause-breathe-let God in.

An arrowhead
    simple and crude
yet, so complex in its wisdom
    from rock to tool
to artifact at my feet.
Radiating its symbology of brother to son
    from loss to love
      to the virtue of hope,
self-love and endorsing life
    I pick it up.

GEMINI TEA

Twin Asian pears, butt up
    on the wooden table
        next to the pine panel
    calico and golden.

Fire in the hearth
    Castor and Pollux
        morning dawns on river-stone.

The lone pine,
    last night's moon pine,
wrapped in a foggy exhale
    of misty mint
that swirls in, off the central coast
    steeping the windowpane
with crystalline dew drops.

PATH

The morning moves through the light
the jacaranda gypsy-like
Caravan fanfare and lavender
trumpets pattern the litter
on the dust settled pathway
it is that mixture of the sublime
and the forlorn that rut the furrow
as it slopes down to the coast
next to the sea with its widening breadth
fanning itself onto the open sand
which once stood high on the slope above
embedded in the fertile soil
or exposed as rocks rich with lichen motif
amidst the scrub oak and mountain laurel
near the base of the jacaranda
next to the path

CENTRAL COAST WASH

Fleet clouds and scented sea breeze
                sends shadow
grey-blue over steel shimmer
like a deep current run
                or canyon bottom
        of the colder depths.
All the while,
                pulling the warm sun
        in and over, taut
        like Native drum skin.
    Central coast wash
                cool and warm
    breathing in and breathing out.

Pine tree sails sway and crack
                in the spin
        and random deer hooves
        splay the dust on worn trails.
    Brown, brown
                patched brown,
    green puddle under
    the drip, drip
                of the garden spigot.
    Central coast wash
                cool and warm
    breathing in and breathing out.

THE PRESENT TENSE

Stiff shoreline breeze
   lays the summer
 short grass south
    both transcendent and immanent
The here and now of paradox.

The pain of powerlessness
  or the ease that comes
    with powerlessness
       a pilgrim's progress.

We have to be willing to suffer
  at a certain level
    for our brothers and sisters.
Both sides of the coin
    here and now.

The sadness and the beauty
    of the fallen, diseased trees
  are a sure example to first growth
    and healthy, old stand pine.

Out here in the world,
  lichen-patch rock and broad oak
    breathe the breath
    of ancient dust.

It often goes unnoticed,
    the present moment,
  where true nature
    is the only nature.

SUN-FACE BUDDHA, MOON-FACE BUDDHA

On the western slope
   of Haleakala in Kula
At Henry Fong Store to buy persimmons.
Dr. Sun Yat Sen walked the hard road
   through the narrow gate
on this high ridge, this incline.
The ocean, thirty-five hundred feet below
   distant and ceaselessly churning
the buttery shoreline from Makena
   to Maalaea Bay.

As in the ocean's depth no wave is born,
   but all is still,
so let the practitioners be still,
   be motionless
and nowhere should they swell.

I wonder if the good doctor
would've kept his mind in his heart
   with Buddha wisdom like this
in his exiled home above the dust?
And if he bought persimmons
   of solitude and simplicity
for one-square inch of free care
while a sea of change fomented
   in South China?

In Gary Snyder's poems
The Persimmons and Mu Chi's Persimmons
   he stills and illuminates
the hard slender limbs of this
slow growing hardwood.

Reminds us that the groves
outlived those of the Great Wall
from both sides, from all ten directions.

And that *those painted persimmons*
the twig and the stalk still on...
sure, cure hunger.

The stuff of life fills the meaning
    represents the symbol
like Hokusai's tsunami painting
    The Great Wave
and its abundant familiarity with calamity.
    Sakura in Sendai
no aura of mindfulness

The nameless is the beginning
    of heaven and earth...
The gate to all mystery.

So many souls like tumbling
    cherry blossoms
in a blizzard of water
flooded Miyagi and Iwate prefectures.

Out of the believers heart
shall flow rivers of living water.
Haka Nasa
    Spirit is the soul of the soul.
The transient and the fragile
    match calamity with serenity
and they will come out
    to see once more the stars.

I take the two persimmons
    from Henry Fong Store
with the twig and stalk still on
    cool to the touch
a burnt orange to the eye
    put them in a bowl
where sunlight and shadow
    crisscross the table,
sun-face Buddha, moon-face Buddha.

FLOWLINE

It used to be said here
I wear myself out staying alive
that coming from a choked heart.

It takes a deep encouragement
transcendent of the horizon of being
      for the hinge of change
        to the gateway to freedom.

It is the best or worst,
sometimes at the same time,
        this interruption from God
that lies at the heart
      of being human.

A fertile ground for faith.

Having our minds
and having the capacity to love
makes it possible to see past
the finger pointing at the moon.

THE PRICE OF EVERTHING SACRED

The morning sky, grey steel
  pall of hushed dust and ash
Pink streaks in the east
Wax paper moon, a speechless snowflake
  dropped on the western night
        the immense silence
            of winter's whisper; Holy
Holy   *Holy*   *Holy*
    everything holy
        like leaves knitting themselves
    into the fabric
                earth.

LUMINOSITY

The quality of earth
        deep-rooted and firm.
Compassion and peace, both solid
    both organic, organic in character.
The earth is my witness.

I saw in the Dharma News today
        that a friend has died,
    a soft and tender heart.
The temptations of strength lie fallow
        in the windless breath
        of the transcendent virtues.

The clouds, lofty and supple,
        expanding and contracting their hope
        anchored in by the horizon line.
    I remind myself not to be too busy
            to understand reality.

Encroaching the farther shore,
        the potential for the future
        as well as the past are revealed.
            Better to be wisdom
    than to know wisdom.

All these notions, so becoming
        so still, in this world of samsara.

The Flame tree clutches its clustered
        red flower in green branches
            vivid, clear
        and wrapped in a silent halo
            in this, the ordinary world.
    It is what is.

Form is luminous and
        partnered with *the great joy*.

I saw in the Dharma News today
        that a friend has died.
The duality of this, the ordinary world,
    Transcendent, transcendent in nature.
The earth is my witness.

SCIMITAR

The way the sun's light lower in the sky
Amber in glow on the up-turned leaves
Silver Dollar eucalyptus---velvet dust
on well-worn roads
The moon visible most of the day, like a pale
Leaf blown against the waxy pate of early fall

You, my mother, rail thin and bankrupt of breath
Told me of your father from your terminal bed
Your frantic search of hospital morgues
Your inability to recognize him from the others
(the attendant having had to point him out)
His head shaved, his body aged beyond his years
The alcohol of the Bunker Hill streets
Drained his love of anything real
I wanted to quote to you, Bhartrhari;
By treading the path of untruth one attains truth
I wanted to tell you of Mark;
For whoever wishes to save his life will lose it
Yet, you are still his little girl, tearful and lost
Filled with the shame and guilt of that image
All these years
Instead I told you that that was not your father
My grandfather
That what you saw was simply the disease
That has cut through our lives
Sure and concise, like a scimitar
The man you knew is in your heart

The pieces we have gathered over these many years
Like apples fallen from the bushel
We hold close to our chests
I did tell you of James;
Faith without works is dead
And you said you knew

The day has turned wan and ashen
And the quick, sharp rhythm
Of the garden rake gathering the tribes
Reveals the slow dance of leaves

PROMISED LAND

A long river from here
     the wise love water
and the kind love mountains
I behave as only as I know how to
when my heart is touched
  all negativity and resistance
subsides.
  practice   give   wisdom
Ample for crossing.

 Long pine forest
       filtered shadows
 counting breaths
walking in the presence of *shen.*

What is it that
     is keeping the stars apart
while the pine moon shines?

Profound peace without limit
     simple and true.

Wake up, we're here
  none of this is going
to mean as much
  as it does right now.

A long trail of seabirds-
   an unbroken chain for fifteen or twenty minutes
streams the break line of morning tide
  -unnoticed.

TAKE EVERYTHING

The river, a deep task,
    passes by well before
the notion that it is coming,
    altering the past
to form the future.

It takes everything
    to wear me out.
It takes a deep confidence-
    a true breath from the heart
to see through the one who sees.

As St. Augustine-
    When you ask, I do not know
    But when you do not, I know.

The river's surface, a roar and an echo,
its underbelly, a swift, silent whisper
    The inherent tarries
in the flow of *the ten thousand things*
and to have a footing on both shores
    is just further testimony that it
takes everything to know nothing.

THE RELINQUISH

The blanched bones
of central coast pine
  sacred with
suffering, grace and God,
parse the light
  of the big blue ocean,
as it lies cradled in the arms
  of the sun and the wind.

The flow of a great paradox;
to be at peace with powerlessness,
  to come full circle,
to stop fighting reality
  and to embrace
the spirit of surrender.

The cacophony of seal barks
  high and low
  swoon and chortle,
a symphony of sorrowful joy.
Corporeal and indolent,
  as they lie complacent
in a mirror of sunshine
   ...just as they are.

GARY SNYDER IS A BLUE JAY

Sea lion bark, well through the night
               chatter and chortle
  all morning long
                  down slope Cambria coast
    atop guano rock
                couple hundred yards out
  in the thick float
        of teeming kelp.

Sunning,
              sanguine bellows & feverish pleas
             trumpets laying claim
  to the metronome of tidal wash
              and the limits of space.

Below the fence line, bordered by fallen
  decayed, bark beetle log rot
    propped rusted metal posts
  stranded barbed wire
The University of California Nature Reserve System
             ecological study area
  and on this side, the non-profit camp
        where Matt and I drink coffee
                       upslope
                     zazen.

The gentle matted slope
  battle worn with central coast pine
            the tops a fortress green
  the lower branches littered with
  flags of stately, quiet moss in surrender.
          Coffee conversation…

A five point buck
          noses through carrizo grass
antlers push up barbed fencing
stealing into the unprotected world
          feasting low-lying branches
                    of California Oak.

I wonder aloud if we will ever see
          Dylan again
                    or Gary Snyder
when a blue jay hops on barbed strand
          like croppt-out rock
     dances to the ridgeline like rip-rap
on switchback
                    perched top of post
          staring out to sea
                    confident-sure
          sense of duty
               like a Sourdough Mountain lookout.

BEAR PAWS AT SUNRISE

Morning in flux
    weaving the out-glow
Into the yawning maw of dawn.
    Heavy-handed
            bear paw dreams.
Weighty is the weight
    that pulls the sun
Over the jagged teeth
            of the eastern ridge.

Full lidded Red Tailed Hawk
    mythic and diffuse
In its faith of a moral compass.
    A predator over its prey,
            anecdotal in its tumbling swoop,
Like shadow stealing sun.

The laws of nature are simple;
Eat or be eaten. Drink
To slake your thirst.
Take what you need,
            leave the rest.
The dawn breaks, the sun sets.

The earth settled in here,
    an echo line from heaven.
A crow's foot of the black to the white
Like a nomenclature stacked between
    a stand of pines—
Or a band of blue absorbing the horizon
    Simple, diametrical
and crowded into this moment.

Mindful of the immediate,
     breath of transcendence,
A fire grows in the mouth of morning.
     Sumac and sage fill the air
And bear tracks in the saw grass
     slowly forgive their impression.

PINECONE

Set down
     as if placed
By the hand of God
Firm, solid and centered
     smack middle
Of the granite paver stone

IMPLICIT

Bleached bone
   trunk of pine past
   stripped of bark
  twinning itself in the stunt
   of an old growth
   central coast pine
Its branches nubbed
   brittle and blackened
  Its adornment of moss
   having fled
Only the top branches fleeced
   only the top branches
   a covey of bird chatter

Ebony and ivory
The dead and the dying
The implicit paradox
   of nature's clutch...
A mercy

THE WRITING TABLE

The slow walk down
    the inclined
soft, sponge-like path
    of chipped coast pine
and tangled scrub oak

Quiet
    almost silent underneath
the steady onshore breeze
    that pushes
the tide in
with a roar of back spray

Descending to
    the ripped pinewood table
      almost flat
    in the afternoon sun

Good enough
    beneath the coiling
standing deadwood
    with the living
       - to write this down

DISCOURSE

Morning doe, two fawn in tow
    stride across the oak leaf chaff
           under the sliver
of a silver moon,
      at lay in lazy repose
against flat purple wisps,
      paint brush on
           bright pink
atop bushy pine peaks
while underfoot a four-point buck
        roots the scrub brush.

COFFEE IN AVILA

I lay my books
        on the café table,
The Lankavatara Sutra
Bede Griffiths, *Return To The Center*
 M Train, Patti Smith
and Edna O'Brien's, *A Pagan Place.*
Reading from truth
        into the reality of the senses.

Duality and projection
        provide no comfort,
to know the self
        springs the eternal,
to further travel from the center,
to beyond existence and non-existence...

Habit-energy is powerful.
Joe Mamas Coffee Shop
        is no reality, gone.
The tide and California's
golden winter light
feather and bathe the coastline,
regardless.
Sands of time and space
blow across the boardwalk.
The eternal and inconceivable
transcends the existence
        and non-existence
of imagined reality.
Tide pools languor in
        low water
 a center for creation.

Truth is not a progress,
        but a return.
Wisdom not improved upon,
        but discoverable
in the breadth of grace.
So this coffee thing,
        Avila is quaint-
Kitsch
boardwalk shops,
        tides and piers,
sea-life and vistas of the infinite.
I walk into *The Hula Hut*
        order a large non-fat latte,
add shot in a mug,
        sit at a table by the window
the tide, like nature's clock
        breaking a rhythm
            and begin to write.

LOVE; A VARIATION

I like to keep some things to myself
Trammeled under by the philosophies du Monde
        hope & suffering
        suffering & hope
The law that is written on our hearts.

Night dreams of radiance & beauty
        impermanent & harmonious
That's the part, the part that revels in
        the transcendence of life,
A complete confidence in the sacredness of the world.

THE EBB & THE FLOW

Dangle,
    dangle down
live big
    and hang fire.
Faithless generosity
    hurts the need,
sparks a flash to the ashes.

Spirit,
    so spirit
waxes wind
    and manifests its kindle
in each and all
    of what is *Here*,
what the body already knows.

ANCIENT HALE

Fog and low clouds
cement the day
   wet on grey.
The valley settled in
its back to the coast
   bathed in sepulchral light
silent and funereal
the highlight of the moment.

It never surprises me anymore
king tide, neap tide,
   boreal winds
that tip the tops
of coniferous forests,
a chorale of whispered truths.
   Or the sun and moon
parabolas insistent on light.

That ancient pull is
groundless and luminous
   a physics of spirit
that drags a limpid line
   to the horizon's edge.
Sails set for voyage
   generous and thin
propel into the alluvial flood
   to the distant shore.

FOR HUANG-PO

The seaward hills nestle in their repose
obstructed by the world and dazed
by the setting sun, will stand in brace
to a night of ten thousand pines.

NO WORK, NO FOOD

Cranes in the tops of tall pines
signify the long flight to transcendence

While walking the steep, curving road
the striking of the evening bell

is as reminder to clear the stones
on the way up

on the road to the sky
through clouds of mists
over peaks
no borders

EVOLUTION

On the embankment
>in the snow

perched a red-crowned crane
>white on white

a stanchion to the creek's
>swift flow.

It takes the whole of life
>*to learn how to live.*

MOUNTAINS AND RIVERS

Self-ablaze
    hence sacred
this occurrence coming of itself
    such as the surf that pounds
the shoreline
    a millstone of glass
that shimmers the central coast
    or the fog that rolls
 the wet dew
    crystalline in its
 collective sigh
    over sumac and sage.
Cascading wisdom
    in this, the mundane flow
transformative, true and tested
    dwelling under the heavenly canopy
the unfolding sky
    mountain, road, monastery.

SAINTS

On Good Friday
   up the seacoast byway pilgrim full
the flat sea glistening
its iridescent shimmer
   just as goldenrod
sways the calm of meadow grass

It's Good Friday
   in Summerland, coastal town
   The Sacred Space
nestled garden-like
   a halcyon to the tempest
of dust that clouds the mind

On Good Friday
teapot on bamboo
   One doesn't leave
the Way to look for the Way
   How true as the sun bathes
our skin in the pure light

It's Good Friday
  and down the Summerland sidewalk
   business bustle
 veiled echo of cicada
   simple turkey with tomato
at *Stackey's Seaside*, we shared

On Good Friday
   the cracks, deep and dark
give the sunshine its depth
The clouds, pillows in pattern

bright on blue, weigh the day
as a reminder of its solemnity

On Good Friday
    up storefront steps
into the shop of Irish pine
    antiques crowded stacked
lined funereal and casket-like
quiet as mourners in the parlor

It's Good Friday
    as we meander over to the park
a shroud of shrubs closes in the world
    quiet pallid the somber of silence
Heavy breath of wet grass
portends the dew of good grace

On Good Friday
    the car climbs Ortega Ridge
to the 192 East Valley Road
 rock walls back road oleander flush
    mountain base path to our old home
the Upper Village Montecito

It's Good Friday
in the market place village above the sea
 Pierre LaFond the sidewalk café life
    high-end Farm cakes
rich in chocolate and cream cheese
melting in streaks in the oppressive sun

On Good Friday
    the afternoon falls forward

to the gate of *Our Lady of Mount Carmel*
Sanctuary silent safe and sorrowful
    the air is heavy and stagnant
The church as museum as mausoleum

It's Good Friday
and the creak of the brittle wooden door
    echoes off adobe wall and oaken beam
Hallowed holiness reveals itself
in the windowed sunbeams of dust particles
    that fall to the cool tiled floor

On Good Friday
in the alcove near the front of the church
    is a kneeler before a small altar
there are flowers in a vase and
    two small lit candles
A statuette of Mary holding her son across her lap
We find ourselves in the courtyard it's three o'clock

In the pall we drive south
the sun sets in the mirror
    the twilight looms ahead
Quiet and sensitive to the hush of eternity
we glide down the coast in search of the tomb
    It's Good Friday

LORD OF FORM

Pine tree
            understory
nag champa fog

afternoon gatha

dry stalk thistle
stiffens the sun breeze
warm wheat grass
bends the arc of horizon

MEDITATION

The fog steams itself
        across the tops
Of kelp beds
        October morn
Sitting practice
        on the mosaic floor
Of the craft room
The sun creeps
        the tree line
        melting thoughts
While the fog inhales
        its last breath

DISTANT SKY

We are still here
    and we have been
here for a while,
marking the wind in lashes
    and the rain in meters,
but it has really been
the long quiet stillness of days,
that endless knot of the mundane
    and the extraordinary,
that draws the distant sky near.

A CULT OF TREES

An avenue of tall pines near my home
Pine pollen blowing in sheets
like late snow on a March blue sky
I have been sitting like a rainforest
zazen- where nothing comes to mind
Waiting for the full moon to rise and
the crane to disembark its perch
The wind takes my problems over the eastern ridge

SHELTER-IN-PLACE
 (under the canopy of heaven)

Red leaves
        of heavenly bamboo
    flutter the light morning sun
Garden stones
        breathe deep
    the last chill of dawn
Small flowers
        yawn wide the advent
     of hummingbird and butterfly
And the back garden
        settles into the
    ten thousand things
Of *tzu-jan,*
        self-ablaze
    this occurrence coming of itself

PANDEM ZAZEN

The garden a slope of color.
Monarch butterfly flutter and bob.
In this time, late spring
Or early summer, I don't know
Seems trouble and sickness rise with the sun.
I sit and wait
Knowing that the moon will
Illuminate the mist that is my mind.

SO WE PRACTICE

Cloud caps and banners of mist
    White crane black rain
Soul wounds show on the skin
    False mind is an illusion
    And true mind is no mind.
Te-shan said
    No mind in work,
    No work in mind.
Seven- day smile
    A noble silence
    The warrior path
        cutting through
This is our practice
This is our breath
        so we practice…

EXILE

Near the *jewel* of the South Coast
Near the end of the pandemic
Across the way
Crystal Cove sealed in, in its vision
       of an America
 very few ever really knew.

I sit in solitude at the koi pond
       reading Liu Tsung-Yuan.
The sun deep in the marine,
  the trees rustling and the fountain
  babbling like a creek marking its way.
The pathway nested with sea life
       crustaceans, shellfish and plants
       embedded fossil-like.

The *sweet dew* still clings
       to the well-tailored garden
 lining either side of the path.
And in this quiet moment
       I am reminded
  to take the teaching
       and strive
 to liberate oneself.

MAHAMUDRA ROOTS

The koi pond again on the blue horizon
        -clear light mind
evermore the *jewel* of the South Coast
The fountain bubbles forth
        bamboo brook luminous
White, orange koi sail beneath
Padma leaves blossoms pink and yellow
Monarch breaches the cracks of paver stones
        Not seeing is the perfect seeing
On the path of solitude and simplicity
the sun wanes bright creeping the shadows
Freedom
        far from a stroke of luck

SQUARE INCH

Emerald aqua and white
fill the tidal wash
the sun at my back
mist and marine on the horizon
warm and cool at the same time
there are no voices or footsteps
only sea rush and birds in the scrub
emptiness fills my mind

CALIFORNIA LIGHT

The deep fog of trees gives way
    to the warm brushstroke of sunrise
Ontology as myth and ritual
Golden breath on oaken slope
    mist of river-stones
Sage musk dusts the amber of hue
Shadows begin to stretch and seep out
        Everything transient
    yet *stillness overcomes heat*
            Everything sacred…

THE TEN THOUSAND THINGS

Scrub oak bramble
    tumbles
        down slope
  to the slow flow writhe
      of the North Fork
  of Matilija Creek
      coiling its way
    between 1931 tunnels
    that connect the Los Padres
National Forest to the Nest
    meandering in its rambling
    pitch and roll of the northeast
Sespe bedrock formation
        tipping and plunging
    the Ventura River bottom
to the breadth
        of the Pacific Ocean
    with its horizon line
      shrouded in shadow
from looming Santa Cruz Island.

This last year with its
              turmoil and sickness
       with its stationary isolation
A rock perched in view
              of time and the
       cosmology of wilderness
       where erosion is effortless
              in its non-movement or freefall
       beneath the canopy of heaven
       leading me to the creek
              to the river
to the ocean
              from boulder
                     to grain of sand.

ON A BENCH OVERLOOKING CAMBRIA COAST

Three turkey vultures windsailing
Over the sandy-like, grassy pitch
Above the slow churning tidal wash.
A torpid coastal front, sure to drop rain,
Vainly tries to gain the sun.
Desires and cares vanish in the quiet.

Straight-sure pine trunk, like paint
Brush green on grey-blue cloudscape,
Flow by. Many of the paths blocked
By fallen deadwood, make it
Essential to share the merit
Of the god rays and the sundogs of what is.

The day skirts the fringe of horizon
And the cool shadow of night
Begins to darken the edges. The metronome
Of tide, is as sure as the moon or the sun.
A reminder that the source is nowhere
And that nowhere has no source.

TAKING REFUGE

From my lookout form is luminous
purple alyssum braiding in between
the golden rocks brought down
from the Sespe formation.

A light breeze dries the
morning rain to a drop of dew.
I often gaze at these rocks
from this vantage point.

Their character and journey evidenced
by their roundness or jagged edges.
Smooth, cracked, or lined faces expose
a spiritual permanence that belies transience.

A passerine, the black phoebe
frequents this performance of stone
as mandala, the flow around him,
the shrill chirp, the vivid reality of life.

Silence, stillness, sunlight
beads on the thread.
Sitting like a stone in the mirror
What is here now is gone.

MOUNTAINS THROUGH PINES

Today the sun a bright beacon
in a field of blue. My grandsons
as gold as twin Asian pears

will visit from the hillside,
Princes of wisdom and light.
We will look into the rivers

of their eyes and it is there
where we will view
mountains through pines.

SCHOLAR OF EMPTINESS

The fog is beginning to lift
    the sun sets regardless
The wild unfurls itself
    over stones in shadow
It is a narrow road
    to a place of peace
Mountains to the sea
    heaven and earth
Why am I lazy?
    Why does this poet
think life is a burden
when
    what all he needs
is to breathe

ON THE PATH

On the trail before
 the sun rises, headed
down so that I can come up,
like breathing under water.
Deadwood line the path
conjuring light in the thick
dark before dawn, a taut
driftwood-like shine fetching
the image of bodies lying end to end.
Oak leaf chaff squeezing below
like stars raising the dead
        to the heavens.

I feel a *dèjá vu* in writing this
        been here before
men meeting in meditation
flawed, fallen, redemption
sitting in silence, in practice.

So much peace in a world of chaos,
So much chaos in a mind desiring peace.

Empty mind, pure quality, the struggle
all the while others die from laughter.

The trail lighted now
as dawn breaks. Heading up,
like a sun touching the clouds,
I notice hoof prints
        buck, doe, and fawn
It seems I'm on the right path.

NOTES

ARROWHEAD
Monsignor Terry Richey, St. Basil's Catholic Church, Los Angeles, California.   For my son, Kyland James

PATH
Chiastic Journey

THE PRESENT TENSE
Monsignor Terry Richey, St. Basil's Catholic Church, Los Angeles, California.   For Monsignor Terry Richey

SUN-FACED BUDDHA, MOON-FACED BUDDHA
Ma-Tsu, (709-788), "Whether healthy or ill, one still practices" - Sun-face Buddha, Moon-face Buddha.

Dr. Sun Yat-sen, *His Life and Achievement*, 1925.

Matthew: 7: 13-14

Jack Kornfield, *The Teachings of the Buddha*, 2004.

Bhagavad Gita 8:12-1

The Zen Works of Stonehouse, translated by Red Pine, 1st translation, 1999.

Gary Snyder, *Left Out in The Rain*, 1986, New Yorker, October 20, 2008.

Katsushika Hokusai, (1760-1849), The Great Wave Off Kanagawa, 1829-1833.

Sakura – Cherry blossom
Fukushima nuclear disaster/Tohoku earthquake and tsunami, March 11, 2011.

Lao Tzu, *Tao Te Ching*, 4th century.

John 7:37-38

Haka Nasa – Transience or fragility of life, immense beauty, tinged with sadness.

Cyprian Consiglio, *Prayer in the Care of the Heart*, 2010.

Alcoholics Anonymous, 1935.

Dante Alighieri, *The Inferno*, 14th century translated by Henry Wadsworth Longfellow, 1867.

FLOWLINE
The Zen Works of Stonehouse, translated by Red Pine, 1st translation, 1999.

LUMINOSITY
Chögyam Trungpa, *Cutting Through Spiritual Materialism*, 1973, *The Myth of Freedom* 1976, *Meditation in Action*, 1991.

James Joyce, *Ulysses*, 1922.

Brachychiton acerifolius, Australian Flame Tree.

THE PRICE OF EVERYTHING SACRED
John 4:10

Allen Ginsberg, *Howl; Footnote*, 1956

PROMISED LAND
Confucius, 551 BC – 479 BC

Shen, Chinese term for spirit, deity

The Zen Works of Stonehouse, translated by Red Pine, 1st translation, 1999.

E. E. Cummings, *Complete Poems; 1904-1962*, 1991.

Chögyam Trungpa, *Meditation in Action*, 1991.

SCIMITAR
Bhartrhari, 5th century Sanskrit poet – grammarian

Mark, 8:35

James, 2:17-18

TAKE EVERYTHING
James Salter, *A Sport and A Pastime*, 1967.

The Zen Works of Stonehouse, translated by Red Pine, 1st translation, 1999.

St. Augustine, 354-430.

Mountain Home, The Wilderness Poetry of Ancient China, David Hinton, 2002.

GARY SNYDER IS A BLUE JAY
Camp Ocean Pines, Cambria, CA.

Gary Snyder, *Turtle Island*, 1974; *Rip Rap; and Cold Mountain Poems*, 1965.

COFFEE IN AVILA
The Lankavatura Sutra, translated by Red Pine, 2012.

Bede Griffiths, *Return to The Center*, 1976
Patti Smith, *M Train*, 2015.
Edna O'Brien, *A Pagan Place*, 1970.

LOVE: A VARIATION
Jeremiah, 31:33

Pema Chodron, *When Things Fall Apart*, 1997.

ANCIENT HALE
The Heart Sutra, translated by Red Pine, 2004

FOR HUANG PO
Huang Po – Died, 850, Zen Master, Tang Dynasty
Most people allow their minds to be obstructed by the world and
then they try to escape from the world. They don't realize that
their mind obstructs the world.

The Diamond Sutra, translated by Red Pine, 2001.

NO WORK, NO FOOD
The Zen principle of No work, No food that was set in
motion by the 4th patriarch, Tao hsin (580-651). The notion
that spiritual work, brings spiritual food is the metaphor
being employed here. The organic nature of this principle
is rooted in a way of living, both in community and in
mind spirit. The oneness that is being nuanced between
the physical world and the metaphysical world expresses
the nature of form is emptiness, emptiness is form and
undeniably is the "now" of daily life.

EVOLUTION
Lucius Annaeus Seneca, (4 BC – AD 65)

MOUNTAINS AND RIVERS
Mountain Home, The Wilderness Poetry of Ancient China,
David Hinton, 2002.

SAINTS
The Sacred Space, Summerland, CA.

The Platform Sutra, The Zen Teaching of Hui-neng, translated by Red Pine, 2006.

SHELTER–IN–PLACE
The Selected Poems of Wang Wei, translated by David Hinton, 2006.

SO WE PRACTICE
Gary Snyder, *Earth Household,* 1969.

Maxine Hong Kingston, *Fifth Book of Peace,* 2004.

The Mountain Poems of Stonehouse, translated by Red Pine, 2nd translation, 2014

Chögyam Trungpa, *Cutting Through Spiritual Materialism,* 1973.

EXILE
"The Jewel" – Laguna Beach

Liu Tsung-Yuan, 773-819 Tang dynasty poet and prose writer.

"Sweet dew" a reference to moisture before it reaches the ground and to the saliva that gathers on the roof of the mouth during meditation.

MAHAMUDRA ROOTS
Mahamudra: "the Great Seal", universal reality of emptiness, non-duality, non-self existence… Mahamudra destroys the nuclear ego.

"Not seeing is the perfect seeing"
Tibetan lama saying attributed to the Buddha.

CALIFORNIA LIGHT
Charles Wright, *Scar Tissue,* 2006.

Lao-Tzu, Verses 40-46.

THE TEN THOUSAND THINGS
The ten thousand things – a distinct property of the Tao
(the Way) and Chan (Zen) in which the ten thousand living
and non-living things are in constant transformation and
non-being is the generative void from which it springs.
This is also central to the Mountains and Rivers tradition
(shan shui) of painting and writing (Shanshui).

The Nest- is a nickname given to Ojai from a 1905 book
of place names. Ojai (*"awha'y*) is from the Ventureno
Chumash word meaning "moon".

ON A BENCH OVERLOOKING CAMBRIA COAST
Red Pine, *The Zen Works of Stonehouse*, 1999, gatha 7.9.

Red Pine, *Zen Roots, The First Thousand Years*, 2020,

Vimalakirti Sutra, Chapter Seven; Beings.

TAKING REFUGE
Chögyam Trungpa, *Cutting Through Spiritualism*, 1973,

Chapter 15. Peter Matthiessen, *The Snow Leopard*, 1978.

MOUNTAINS THROUGH PINES
Red Pine, *The Zen Works of Stonehouse*, 1999.

ACKNOWLEGMENTS

GRATEFUL to my dear Christine, forever a patient font of spiritual love and to my family, for their love, assistance and presence. To Phoebe MacAdams for her long friendship from the valley to the hills beyond. Terry Bozzio, a spiritual kinship kindled by the spark of passion and collaboration. Doug Knott, for filling the room with adventure. Matt Brown and Jim Schicker, sutra and sangha brothers.

GASSHŌ to the Ojai Poetry Series, love and respect to my dear friends and coordinators, Judy Oberlander and Crystal Eckels Davis. And to the poets that cross paths on trails of truth, Vincent Mowery, Elizabeth Dinkins, Phil Taggart, Marsha de la O and Laure-Anne Bosselaar. Special thanks to Tamara Miller Davis.

THE ARTISTS Beatrice Wood, whose presence and lively conversation, I can still feel and hear. Jane Shanahan, your generosity and proficiency set the stage. Timm Sinclair, brother, we are still standing after all these years. Daggi Wallace, I am awed by your talent.

THE PRINTERS Dave Reeser, Blue Jay Ink, Jim Brent, Museum Quality Art Services, Norman Clayton, Classic Letterpress, I know fortune and grace are equal to the expressions of words and art. I am in the best of company.

SHAMANS AND TEMPLES The real -life encounters that shaped process into style. Gary Snyder, W.S. Merwin, Michael McClure, Sam Hamill, Allen Ginsberg, Lawrence Ferlinghetti, William S. Burroughs, Jeff Grimes, Mark Salerno, Sean Heaney, Art Beebe, Steve Diamond, Claire Rabe, Laurence Malone, Freya Manfred, Tom Clark and Lewis MacAdams. John Martin, Black Sparrow Press and Noel Young, Capra Press. Peace and praise.

Monsignor Terry Richey, David Hinton, Chögyam Trungpa, Shunryu Suzuki and Ted Berrigan. The works of Peter Matthiessen and Edna O'Brien are a reminder to me that *vers libre* often takes place in the moment, right where you are.

This brings me to the temples and an acknowledgement of appreciation to the locations of where these poems were written. Cam-zendo, my home in Camarillo, Ca. where I practice, read and write. Cambria, Ca. and non-profit, Camp Ocean Pines, forever indebted. The seacoast village of Avila, San Luis Obispo County, Ca. Montecito and Summerland, neighbors and forever home. Beloved Ojai, Rose Valley, the North Fork of Matilija Creek, and the hamlet nestled up against the Topa Topas. The beginning, the middle... Laguna Beach, a jewel and my exile. Let me end where I started, in gratitude. The last line of the Heart Sutra.

Gate, gate, paragate, parasangate, bodhi svaha

Poems featured in Gandy Dancer Press Broadsides

Arrowhead, 2010, w/ Jane Shanahan, artist and graphic designer

Flowline, 2015, w/ Timm Sinclair, artist and graphic designer

No Work, No Food, 2017

Path, 2017

Sun-Faced Buddha, Moon-Faced Buddha Scroll, 2017 w/ Terry Bozzio, musician, composer, and artist

Meditation, 2018, photograph by Timm Sinclair

Distant Sky, 2019, photograph by Todd Griese

Gary Snyder Is A Blue Jay, 2019, w/ Jim Brent Museum Quality Art Services

The Present Tense, 2020, photograph by Todd Griese

A Cult Of Trees, 2020, photograph by Todd Griese

Shelter-In-Place, 2020, photograph by Todd Griese

Pandem Zazen, 2020, photograph by Todd Griese

Central Coast Wash, 2020, photograph by Todd Griese

Luminosity Scroll, 2020

So We Practice, 2021, w/ Jim Brent Museum Quality Art Services

afternoon gatha, 2021, photograph by Todd Griese

The Ten Thousand Things, 2021, photograph by Todd Griese

California Light, 2021, photograph by Todd Griese

Cambria Coast (On A Bench Overlooking Cambria Coast), 2021, photograph by Todd Griese

Evolution Scroll, 2021

Mountains Through Pines, 2021, photograph by Gene Talmadge

Poems featured on Audio Compilation

No Work, No Food, A Journey Along Spiritual Lines Production, 2017, A collaborative collection of audio Compositions with legendary musician, composer and artist, Terry Bozzio.

Arrowhead
Scimitar
Central Coast Wash
Sun-Faced Buddha, Moon-Faced Buddha
Coffee In Avila
Flowline
Take Everything
Mountains And Rivers
The Present Tense
No Work, No Food
The Price Of Everything Sacred
Promised Land
The Relinquish

Broadsides and CD available @gandydancerpress.net

ABOUT THE AUTHOR

Todd Griese is a poet and the publisher at Gandy Dancer Press, a small press dedicated to and specializing in Collaborative and Mixed-Media Arts. He has published thirty-five Art Broadsides since 2010.

Todd is also the author of *Spiritual Lines* (2009) and *North Fork* (2018).

North Fork was written in response to the Thomas Fire that consumed Ventura and Santa Barbara counties in California late 2017 into early 2018. *North Fork* was also part of the Ojai Valley Museum exhibition, *Trial By Fire*.

Todd's published work includes collaborative expressions of poetry, art, music in various forms; books, prints, canvas broadsides and recorded compositions. His collaborators include artist/graphic designer, Jane Shanahan (2009-2012), artist/graphic designer, Timm Sinclair (2015-2017), and award-winning pastel artist, Daggi Wallace (2018).

In 2017, Todd Griese and legendary drummer/composer/artist Terry Bozzio embarked on a project that produced an album, *(No Work, No Food)*, seven broadsides, including a Japanese scroll *(Sun-Face Buddha, Moon-Face Buddha)*, two live shows (Arts Alive 2017), and a gallery installation, *(A Part of the Landscape, A Part of the Human Condition)*, the Blackboard Gallery, Studio Channel Islands, Camarillo, California.

www.ingramcontent.com/pod-product-compliance
Lightning Source LLC
Chambersburg PA
CBHW031250120626
46545CB00007B/2739